Learner Services

Please return
on or before
the last date
stamped below

guggenheim *bilbao*

photographs by jeff goldberg

PRINCETON ARCHITECTURAL PRESS NEW YORK

julie v. iovine

IF IT HAD NOT already happened, the creation of the Guggenheim Museum in Bilbao, Spain, would seem almost impossibly improbable. Who could have anticipated that a proud, former shipbuilding town and an ambitious and savvy American museum director would join forces to create a work of architecture lauded as one of the century's most significant? It all appeared to fall into place as effortlessly as destiny itself, bringing together such unlikely players as the Basques of Spain, Guggenheim director Thomas Krens in New York, and Frank Gehry of Los Angeles, the reigning genius of American architecture in the 1990s.

Perhaps it was no accident that fiercely independent Bilbao, once the salted cod fish capital of the world, would turn out to be the ideal site for Gehry, who was taunted as "fish-face" as a child before transforming the piscine insult into a totem of ebullient creativity in adulthood.

The Bilbao museum doesn't look at all like a fish. In fact, it purposefully defies all easy descriptions. Stretched out along the Nervión River in an industrial neighborhood long past its prime, its quivering titanium flanks gleam when viewed from the surrounding hills or when glimpsed at the ends of streets lined with polite nineteenth-century buildings. Calvin Tompkins, in the *New Yorker*, called it first "a fantastic dream ship" and then a "prehistoric beast"; Joachim Pissarro, in the British art magazine *Apollo*, compared it to the great Byzantine cathedral Hagia Sophia, while in the *New York Times Magazine* Herbert Muschamp invoked the mercurial brilliance of Marilyn Monroe.[1]

While critics and visitors grope for ways to describe the museum, one thing is amply clear: that it was Thomas Krens's intention from the start to provoke Gehry into rethinking the very concept of the contemporary art museum in the hopes of creating a twentieth-century landmark. In *Frank Gehry Talks about Architecture and Process*, Gehry recalled presenting a version of the museum's atrium, one of its most distinctive features, that was boxy and square only to have Krens egg him on to something more daring: "Do something else. Take it on. Make it better than Wright," Krens encouraged.[2]

As a result, the museum's soaring atrium space—one-and-a-half times as high as Frank Lloyd Wright's rotunda in Manhattan's Guggenheim—has become one of the most talked about features of the 257,000-square-foot museum. "It is impossible to describe the emotion of this space," wrote the *Los Angeles Times* architecture critic Nicolai Ourousoff in his review of 2 June 1997, five months before the official opening that October. "It is here, in the atrium, that the building comes to life. Its undulating, erotic form twists up toward the sky, as if to suck the visitor up into some wonderful dream."[3]

The space actually rises 138 feet but appears even loftier due to an entry procession that first leads the visitor, like Orpheus, down a full level on a grand stair. Within the atrium and overhead, stairs, walkways, and glassed-in elevators peel off in fragments and split overhead around curvaceous plaster pylons to reveal broad views of the river. While the exfoliating titanium strips of metal that crown the atrium's exterior are routinely referred to simply as the petals of a blossoming rose, Russian constructivists, German expressionists, Italian futurists, and Fritz Lang's *Metropolis* have all been invoked to describe the atrium's interior (Gehry himself told the artist Coosje van Bruggen that he'd been partially inspired by Henri Matisse's paper cut-outs). The standarization-defying shape of the building was made possible by Gehry's pioneering work with a three-dimensional computer modeling system known as CATIA, a technology more commonly used in the aerospace industry. (Gehry himself doesn't work the computers, claiming that he can only bear to look at a computer screen for a maximum of four minutes.)

The galleries, comprising 112,000 square feet of exhibition space, lead off the atrium and have been treated more analytically than emotionally. The largest, referred to as the "boat" (during construction, the builders came up with other handy names such as "boot," "cobra," and "Zorro" to help them find their way around these unconventional spaces) measures 450 feet long by 80 feet wide and may qualify as the largest gallery for art in the world. Krens clearly wanted it that way, and when Gehry suggested adding two walls to reduce the scale, he rejected the idea. This heroic hall is home to the most monumental art works, from Richard Serra's 104-foot *Snake*, three curving walls of rusted steel weighing 174 tons that was specially commissioned for the center of the gallery, to Claes Oldenburg's motorized *Knife Ship* in full swing at the far end. The building has conventional spaces as well. Of its nineteen principal galleries, more than half are traditional rooms that make little reference to the commotion in the atrium and on the exterior. These galleries hold the Guggenheim's collection of modernist classics by the likes of Pablo Picasso, Georges Braque, Fernand Léger, Joán Miró, and Vasily Kandinsky. Six galleries are more audaciously shaped—the ones with the nicknames—but have been criticized for intrusive lighting systems (in one dedicated to works by Sol LeWitt), for awkward proportions, and, in the Anselm Kiefer gallery, for having had its curved walls straightened up. (Gehry himself was reportedly disappointed that workmen took it upon themselves to "correct" the tilted walls).

But it is the exterior of the building that has become its most steadfast beacon of architectural bravado. The swoop and shine of it—and especially the way that it reaches under a bridge only to thrust itself up on the other side—has riveted the attention of the world and turned an unlikely gambit into an architectural wonder. It was in 1991 that representatives of the Basque government first approached Thomas Krens with the idea of a museum as the keystone to a $1.5 billion urban redevelopment plan for Bilbao. Their agreement called for the Basques to construct and support a museum to be staffed and operated by the Guggenheim. After a brief flirtation with the idea of an architectural competition, Frank Gehry was awarded the commission.

Before the museum officially opened in October 1997, critics scoffed at projections that five-hundred-thousand tourists a year would journey to Bilbao to visit a museum. As it turned out, over 1,360,000 visitors came in the first year alone, and the Guggenheim Bilbao has since established itself as one of the foremost architectural pilgrimages of the century.

notes

1. Calvin Tompkins, "The Maverick." *New Yorker* (7 July 1997); Joachim Pissarro, "Gehry's Guggenheim Museum in Bilbao," *Apollo* (December 1997); Herbert Muschamp, "The Miracle in Bilbao," *New York Times Magazine*, 7 Sept 1997.

2. Frank Gehry, *Frank Gehry Talks about Architecture and Process* (New York: Rizzoli, 1999).

3. Nicolai Ourousoff, review, *Los Angeles Times*, 2 June 1997.

"The greatest building of our time."   —Philip Johnson

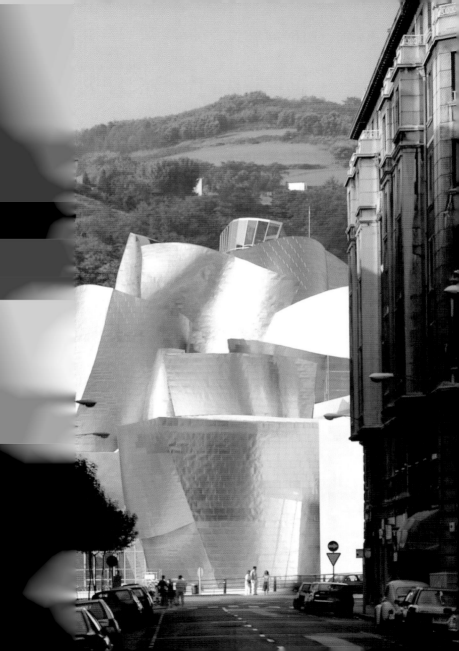

"Do something else. Take it on. Make it better than Wright."   —Thomas Krens

"The container and the contained, the art and the architecture, are one thing, made for each other."

—Ada Louise Huxtable

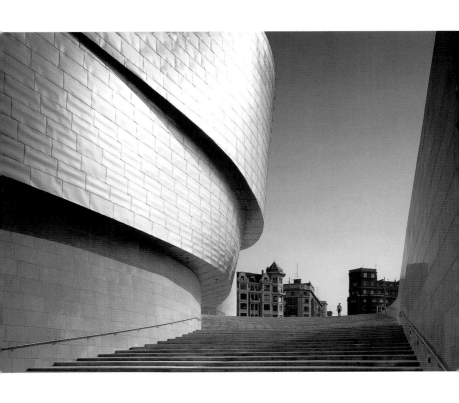

"Twentieth century artists have given us so much and no museum has caught up to it. This is a beginning."

—Ellsworth Kelley

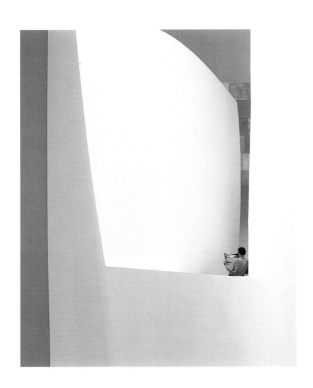

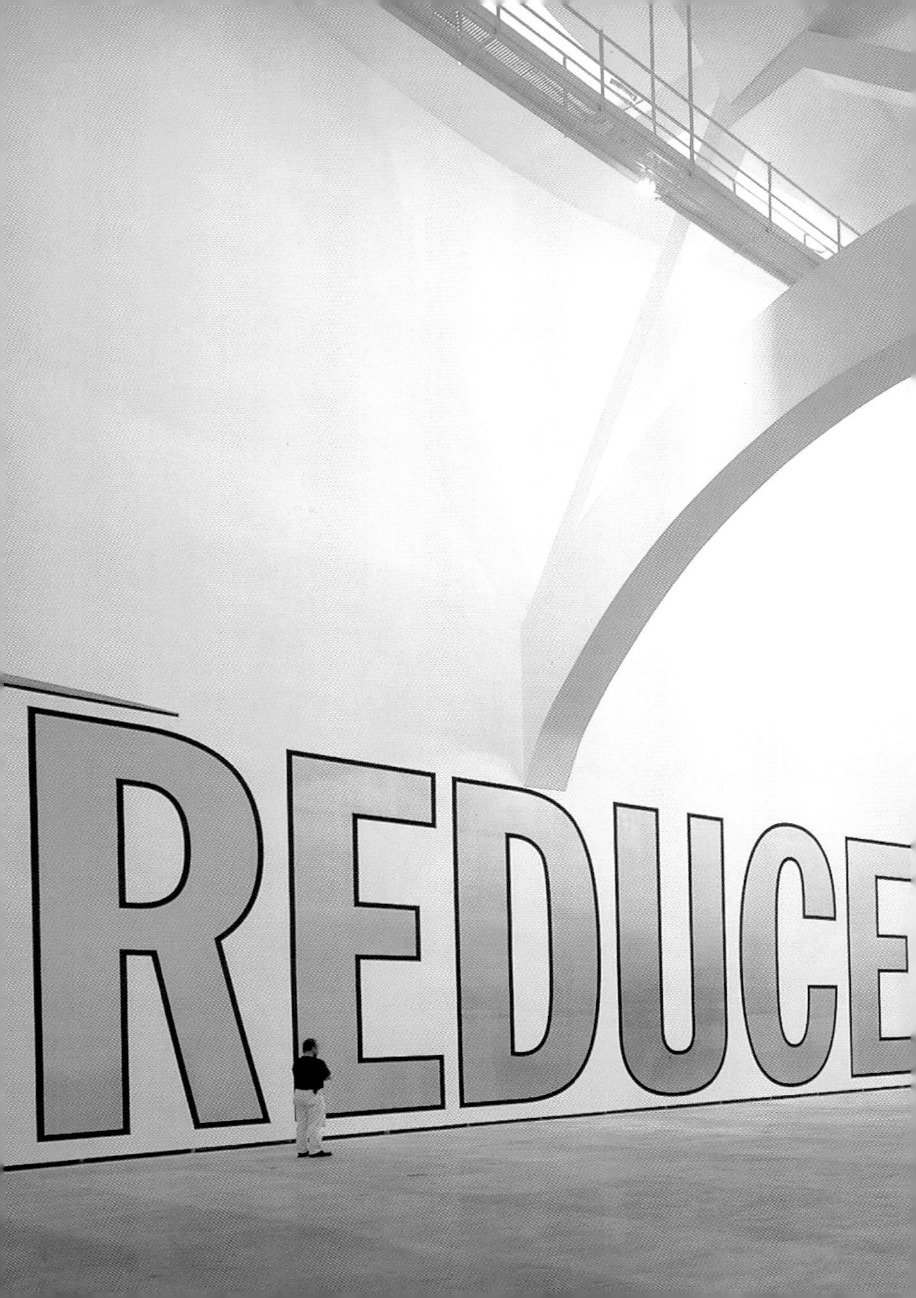
REDUCE

"A part of me says 'What the hell are you guys all excited about?'"   —Frank Gehry

"Short of insisting that no pictures at all be shown, Wright could not have gone much further to create a structure sublime in its own right but ridiculous as a museum of art."

—Lewis Mumford

"The eye encounters no abrupt change, but is gently led and treated as if at the edge of the shore watching an unbreakable wave—or is that too fancy a phrase?" —Frank Lloyd Wright

"It is not the most practical building in the world—but neither, one suspects, is the Pantheon." —Peter Blake

"We have finished with doors and windows. I am tired of them. The building of the future will be 'organic architecture.'"

—*Frank Lloyd Wright*

"I have no doubt that your building will be a great monument to yourself." —Hilla von Rebay

"*I am so full of ideas for our museum that I am likely to blow up or commit suicide unless I can let them out on paper.*"

—*Frank Lloyd Wright*

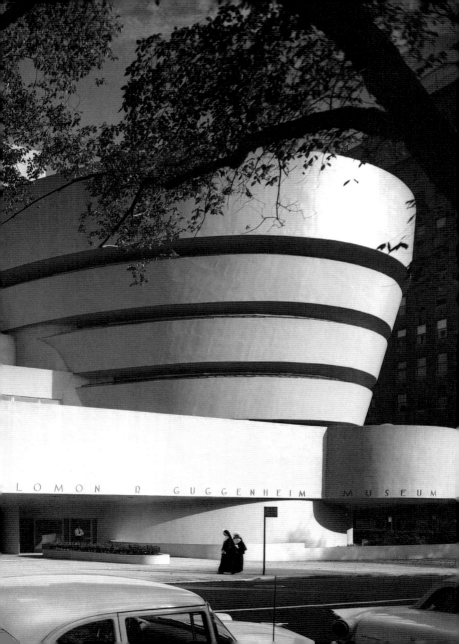

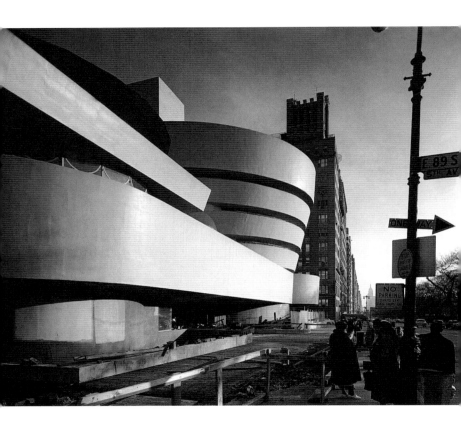

"short of insisting that no pictures at all be shown, Wright could not have gone much further to create a structure sublime in its own right but ridiculous as a museum of art."[9]

While critics continued to air their opinions that Wright's Guggenheim overwhelmed the art within, the public flocked to the building, anticipating the day when museums would operate as agoras for hanging out as much as forums for hanging art. In a Gallup poll conducted just one year after the museum opened, surveyors found that nearly four out of every ten visitors to the museum came just to see the building, while only 5 percent came just to view the collection.[10]

Ever prescient, Wright's concern about copycat designs was also on the mark: within three months of the museum's opening, the Daitch-Shopwell chain introduced a circular supermarket with a seven-story ramp.

notes

1. Bruce Brooks Pfeiffer, ed., *Frank Lloyd Wright: The Guggenheim Correspondence* (Carbondale, IL: Southern Illinois University Press, 1986), 112.
2. "Museum Building to Rise as Spiral," *New York Times*, 10 July 1945.
3. Pfeiffer, ed., *Guggenheim Correspondence*, 4.
4. Ibid., 41.
5. Quoted by Peter Blake in "The Guggenheim: Museum or Monument," *Architectural Forum* (December 1959).
6. Neil Levine, *The Architecture of Frank Lloyd Wright* (Princeton: Princeton University Press, 1996), 327.
7. Sandra Knox, "21 Artists Assail Museum Interior," *New York Times* 12 December 1956.
8. Frank Lloyd Wright, "The Solomon R. Guggenheim Memorial," *Architectural Record* 123 (May 1958).
9. Lewis Mumford "The Sky Line: What Wright Hath Wrought," *New Yorker* (5 December 1959).
10. Robert A. M. Stern, Thomas Mellins, and David Fishman, *New York 1960: Architecture and Urbanism between the Second World War and the Bicentennial* (New York: Monacelli Press, 1995), 820.

work on the project slowed drastically due both to doubts that it could be constructed that were expressed by the city's Department of Buildings and in response to Guggenheim's death in November 1949. With her patron gone, Rebay's days at the foundation were numbered. By March 1952 she was replaced by James Johnson Sweeney, a more professional museum administrator motivated by straightforward notions about presenting art who was not prone to flights of architectural fancy. There was talk among the trustees of replacing Wright and starting the museum project from scratch.

Apparently unfazed, Wright revised his working drawings and began to confront the thirty-two violations found by the Building Commission when the plans were first filed. The trustees, to their credit, stuck with Wright and a building permit was finally issued on 23 May 1956.

The design was now fair game for all comers. The *New York Times* launched an opening salvo in an editorial of 8 May 1956. Describing themselves as collectively "aghast," the editors stated that "The net effect, if we may say so, will be precisely that of an oversized and indigestible hot cross bun." Hilton Kramer, then the managing editor of *Arts* magazine, complimented the building as architecturally grand but complained of its small regard for paintings and sculpture. Then the artists themselves stepped forward, sending an open letter to the trustees in which they described the interiors as "not suitable for a sympathetic display of painting and sculpture." Among the distinguished signatories were Milton Avery, Willem de Kooning, Philip Guston, Franz Kline, Robert Motherwell, and Jack Tworkov.[7]

Wright, ever confident in his mission, rose above the fray and issued a statement in May 1958 that would turn out to be his last written words on the museum, describing his efforts as "a genuine intelligent experiment in museum-culture."[8] He died on 9 April 1959, six months before the building opened to the public and, ironically, five months before a survey of five-hundred leading architects ranked it as the eighteenth wonder of American architecture.

Lewis Mumford, writing his Sky Line column in the *New Yorker*, called the completed museum "a Procrustean structure," adding that

Before the month was out, Wright had a contract guaranteeing him a 10 percent fee for a $750,000 building on an undetermined site. It would be, along with Philip Goodwin and Edward Durell Stone's Museum of Modern Art (1938–39), one of the first significant commissions for modern architecture in New York City.

Wright was ebullient at the first press conference, held in July of 1945 at the Plaza hotel, at which he announced his preliminary design and revealed a working model. Working drawings were soon completed for a pre-stressed reinforced concrete structure—in the shape of an inverted ziggurat—topped with a glass dome and lined on the open interior with a spiraling ramp in place of traditional floors. The walls supporting the art works would be tilted, like easels; lighting would be almost exclusively natural. Wright described the building as an indestructible spring: "When the first atom bomb lands on New York it will not be destroyed," he declared at the press conference, "it may be blown a few miles up into the air, but when it comes down it will bounce!"[5]

Immediately after its unveiling, artists began to warn Rebay that the building as designed would never do for showing their work. László Moholy-Nagy and Rudolf Bauer, intimate friends of the curator, both advised her of their apprehension. Rebay herself had already expressed concern about the hike visitors would be required to make up Wright's proposed ramp: more than a quarter-mile at a 3 percent grade. "Never speak of a 'climb' in the new building," cautioned Wright, (who envisioned visitors taking the elevator to the top and heading down). "You only take an easy walk slightly—very slightly—uphill." In 1944, a full-scale review of the plans was ordered. "While I have no doubt that your building will be a great monument to yourself," Rebay wrote, still concerned in January 1945, "I cannot visualize how much (or how little) it will do for the paintings." Her friends even suggested she get a second opinion on the interiors from another architect, perhaps Mies van der Rohe.[6]

In fact, by the time it went into construction Wright had prepared six complete sets of plans and 749 new drawings. Throughout the late forties

Throughout the sixteen years it took to get built, the project was scrutinized and appraised, flattered by politicians, reviled by artists, and supported through thick and thin by the Guggenheim clan and its patriarch, Solomon R. Guggenheim. Midway through the agonizing process, Guggenheim fended off skeptics, stating emphatically that "the House of Guggenheim never goes back on its word—the museum will be built. You should pay no attention to what people say."[1] Guggenheim's words held true, though neither he nor Wright lived to see the building completed.

If Guggenheim sounded a bit like Oz telling Dorothy and friends not to look at that mere man behind the curtain, he had reason for confidence. Wright was a wizard. His vision of an organic architecture that would erupt into a "new type of treasury for works of art, one that would be a haven of refuge for city dwellers" was leavened with a healthy dose of pragmatism. "I hope we can get this built before some department store adopts the idea," he confided to a *New York Times* reporter in 1945.[2]

The trajectory of opinions, reactions, and objections that gained dizzying momentum through the conception, development, and construction of Wright's most famous building offers a kind of kaleidoscopic perspective on the forty-year-old museum, a perspective almost as riveting as the view from the top of the building's spiraling ramp.

The idea for the museum originated with Baroness Hilla von Rebay, curator of the Solomon R. Guggenheim Foundation, a passionate collector of non-objective art, and a believer in trendy notions of spiritual enlightenment. "I need a fighter, a lover of space, an originator, a tester and a wise man. . . . I want a temple of spirit, a monument!" she wrote in her first communication with Wright, on 1 June 1943.[3]

Needless to say, the seventy-six-year-old Wright was interested, and soon the architect and the curator were exchanging letters inflamed with visionary language. She wrote: "With infinity and sacred depth create the dome of spirit: expression of the cosmic breath itself—bring light to light!" He answered in kind: "Anything more modern, less stuffy and conventional, you have never seen. Nor anything so ideal for your purpose. So much all these things that you may be at first shocked or offended."[4]

solomon r. guggenheim museum, new york

julie v. iovine

FROM ITS INCEPTION in 1943, the Solomon R. Guggenheim Museum has thrived on controversy. Initially, excitement overflowed as New York City awaited its first—and as it turned out only—building by the country's most famous architect, Frank Lloyd Wright. By August 1956, when the builders finally broke ground at the museum's Fifth Avenue site—between Eighty-ninth and Ninetieth streets—anticipation had been honed into the received wisdom that still largely applies today: here is a monumental work of contemporary architecture almost entirely indifferent to the needs of contemporary artists.

PUBLISHED BY
Princeton Architectural Press
37 East Seventh Street
New York, NY 10003

For a catalog of books published by Princeton
Architectural Press, call toll free 800.722.6657
or visit www.papress.com

EDITOR: Mark Lamster
BOOK AND COVER DESIGN: Sara E. Stemen

Photographs on pages 11, 12–3, 21, 28–9, and
30–1 of Guggenheim Museum Bilbao by Ralph
Richter © Ralph Richter/architektur photo/Esto

ACKNOWLEDGMENTS: I would like to thank my
colleagues at Esto Photographics, especially Kent
Draper and Laura Bolli; Mary Doyle and Mike
Kimines of TSI for their help in preparing these
images; and Mark Lamster for his support from start
to finish.   —Erica Stoller

SPECIAL THANKS: Ann Alter, Eugenia Bell, Jane
Garvie, Caroline Green, Clare Jacobson, Leslie Ann
Kent, Lottchen Shivers, and Jennifer Thompson of
Priceton Architectural Press
                              —Kevin C. Lippert, Publisher

For the licensing of all images, contact
Esto Photographics. Fine art reproductions
of Stoller prints are available through the
James Danziger Gallery.

PRINTED IN CHINA

LIBRARY OF CONGRESS
CATALOGING-IN-PUBLICATION DATA
IS AVAILABLE FROM THE PUBLISHER.

guggenheim *new york*

photographs by ezra stoller

PRINCETON ARCHITECTURAL PRESS NEW YORK